The Aquarian Runes

The ancient art of runecasting enters the Aquarian Age.

by
Zera Starchild of An

Doorway Publications
16428 Tee Place
Weed, CA 96094
916-938-1069

© 1993 by Zera Starchild. All rights reserved. No part of this book may be reproduced by any means and in any form without written permission from the publisher, except for brief quotations embodied in literary articles or reviews.

Printed by Griffin Printing; Penny Hancock
Sacramento, CA
First printing 1993
10 9 8 7 6 5 4 3 2 1

ISBN 0-9632970-2-3

Cover illustration, photographs, graphic design and layout by: Christof Schneider-Reuter a.k.a. Timotek

Our thoughts and imagination are our only limits.

CONTENTS

PAGE

Quick Reference Guide.................... a

The Story of the Runes................. 1

Why Divination works..................... 3

How to use the Aquarian Runes........... 5

Questions............................... 7

Changing Limiting Beliefs................ 28

Creating Your Reality.................... 32

The Aquarian Runes Definitions........... 43

Quick Reference Guide

Rune		Page	Rune		Page	Rune		Page
Completion		44	Inner Communication		60	Radical Discontinuity		75
Going Within		45	Self-nurturance		62	Right Direction		76
The Shadow		47	Death		64	Partnership		78
Joy		49	Movement		66	Eyes Open		79
The Bridge		51	Messages		68	Stand Still		81
Termination New Beginnings		53	Wholeness		70	Harvest		82
Destiny		55	Limitation		71	Let go		83
Growth		56	Fulfillment		72			
Disconnectedness		58	Breakthrough		74			

<u>Note:</u> Some of the runes shown above have reversed positions, not pictured here. For a reversed rune definition, find the rune's upright position in the quick reference guide, and refer to the following page.

The Story of the Runes

The runes are a sacred alphabet once used by ancient Germanic people as a divination tool. They were introduced into Europe during the last great Ice Age, between 120,000 BC and 10,000 BC, by a tribe from northern Scandinavia.

The word rune means "a mystery or holy secret that is whispered." Over the centuries rune knowledge spread throughout northern and central Europe, and was carried by the Vikings from the Arctic and New Foundland to the Mediterranean.

Throughout their history, the runes have been reinterpreted many times to accommodate man's expanding awareness. Now, humanity stands in astrological understanding at the dawn of the Aquarian Age. This is the age when mankind learns to live in peace and harmony.

The Aquarian Runes honor the significance of these times, and offer new definitions from the perspective that we are not victims of fate, but creators of our reality.

You are the master of your destiny. Use the Aquarian Runes to help you create the most joyous life you can imagine.

Why Divination Works

The essence of each human being is spirit. As spirit we are conscious energy living in a world where energy solidifies to become matter.

Our thoughts, feelings and beliefs are also energies that, like magnets, attract like energies to them. This phenomenon is called resonance. Because of resonance our outer reality always reflects what's inside us, and our inner reality creates what we experience.

When you pull a rune from a bag, or a tarot card from a deck, you are working with the law of resonance. The knowledge symbolized by the oracle reflects the divine wisdom that is within you. In such a way divination is a kind of game you play with two parts of yourself... the you searching for truth and the you which knows the answer.

Every civilization on earth has used some form of divination. In the past, the art was reserved for only those believed to possess "supernatural" powers. As humanity awakens to a higher level of consciousness, it's time to recognize divination as a self-empowerment tool which anyone can use. Wisdom is power, and there is no greater power than knowing one's self.

How to Use the Runes

After putting together the rune set in this book you are ready to begin. You may of course use your own rune set if you already have one.

Put your runes into their bag. For each question you ask, draw one rune. After your reading return the card to the bag.

Start by getting acquainted with the language of the Aquarian Runes with a one rune reading. Simply ask spirit, "Where am I now in my life?" and pull one rune for your answer. Look up the definition in the Aquarian Runes Definitions (page 43).

The runes can answer any question that does not require a yes or no response. You'll find they work best when you compose your own questions, but some questions have been provided to get you started.

Use these until you become familiar with how best to consult the runes. You'll find that any divination system is only as effective as the questions you ask.

Once you're familiar with the Aquarian Runes you can use them for daily guidance on any issue. This book will also teach you how to use the runes and the moon to create the life you desire. If you're ready, let's begin.

Clarity

Where am I now in my life?

 notes:

Where am I going?

 notes:

What is my divine focus at this time?

 notes:

What is my divine path?

 notes:

What's going to happen next?

 notes:

What is life teaching me now?

 notes:

Problem Solving

Use these questions when you have a problem.

What should I do to resolve my problem?

 notes:

What should I focus on to see this situation in the highest light?

 notes:

What am I learning from this situation?

 notes:

What will be the outcome of this situation?

 notes:

Resolving Conflicts

Use these questions to resolve problems in relationships.

Why have I created this conflict with _____?

☐ notes:

What am I learning from this conflict?

☐ notes:

What is my path to resolve this conflict with _____?

 notes:

What should I focus on as I walk this path?

 notes:

What will be the outcome of this situation?

 notes:

Creating Happy Relationships

What should I focus on to create greater harmony in my relationship with _____?

 notes:

What is my truest desire concerning relationships at this time?

 notes:

What should I focus on to attract a loving partner into my life?

 notes:

What does my spirit want me to create next in my relationship with
_____?

 notes:

How can I maintain loving ties with
_____ while continuing to move forward on my path?

 notes:

The Life You Desire

You have the power to create the life you desire.

Here are some questions designed to connect you with your power.

What should I focus on to claim my power?

 notes:

What should I focus on so that I do not give my power away?

 notes:

What should I focus on to tap into my power of creativity?

 notes:

What should I focus on to create Heaven on Earth in my life?

 notes:

Opening to Receive

What should I focus on to receive more _____ in my life?
(Fill in the blank with each word below, and pull a rune for each word.)

Love   _____Rune notes:

Peace   _____Rune notes:

Joy   _____Rune notes:

Light   _____Rune notes:

Wealth   _____Rune notes:

Health   _____Rune notes:

Abundance _____ Rune notes:

Self-love   _____ Rune notes:

Fulfillment   _____Rune notes:

Opportunity   _____Rune notes:

Money   _____Rune notes:

All that I desire   _____Rune notes:

Heaven on Earth   _____Rune notes:

Other   _____ Rune notes:

Your Path to Walk

What is my path to spiritual breakthrough?

 notes:

What is my path to greater clarity?

 notes:

What is my path to greater self-love?

 notes:

What is my path to receive all that I desire?

 notes:

Receiving Money

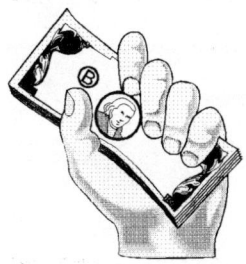

What do I need to focus on to create more money in my life?

 notes:

What should I do next to receive more money?

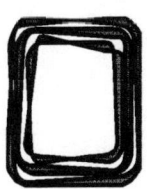 notes:

What am I learning from my current money situation?

 notes:

What will happen next with my money situation?

 notes:

Receiving Love

What should I focus on now to receive more love in my life?

 notes:

What should I focus on to receive a true partner in my life?

 notes:

What should I focus on to balance my relationship with my partner?

 notes:

What am I learning from my current relationship situation?

 notes:

Receiving Good Health

What should I focus on now to become healthier?

 notes:

What should I do next to become healthier?

 notes:

What is the lesson behind the health problem I've been having?

 notes:

Receiving My Self

What should I focus on to feel the power of my Higher Self?

 notes:

What should I focus on to see with the vision of my Higher Self?

 notes:

What should I focus on to act with all the power of my Higher Self?

 notes:

What is my path to live my fullest potential?

 notes:

Changing Limiting Beliefs

Our beliefs shape our reality. If our beliefs are limiting we may be shortchanging ourselves and creating less for ourselves than we deserve.

Working with the Aquarian Runes can help you replace limiting beliefs with more positive ones.

The following is a list of some commonly held "negative" beliefs that can hold you back from creating a joyous life. For any of these beliefs you hold and want to change, pull three runes to answer these questions:

- What is my next step to change this belief?
- What should I focus on as I take this step?
- What will be the result of taking this step?

Beliefs You're Ready to Change

- "I won't be able to create what I want."
- "I can't have what I want."
- "I'll never be able to make enough money to live abundantly."
- "I'll never be able to create a joyous life for myself."
- "I'll never have a fulfilling relationship."
- "I'll always be alone."
- "I'll never be able to quit my job and do what I love."
- "Whenever something good happens in my life, something has to spoil it."
- "The men in my life always leave me."
- "The women in my life always leave me."
- "There's always a price you pay for freedom."
- "I'll never get out of debt."

Feel free to add to this list with other beliefs you'd like to change.

Questions To Help You Change Limiting Beliefs

What should I focus on to change my thoughts, so that I may create a more joyous life for myself?

 notes:

What should I focus on now to shift my thinking from doubt and fear to joy and abundance?

 notes:

What should I focus on to move through my fears?

 notes:

What should I focus on to release my ego's attachment to a particular outcome?

 notes:

What is my path to live life as an unlimited being?

 notes:

What should I focus on to walk this path?

 notes:

The Creation Cycle

You create your reality in every moment, by your thoughts, feelings and beliefs. Most of this process happens on an unconscious level, but there is a way for you to become more aware of this process as it unfolds in your life.

Earth's ancient civilizations studied the movements of celestial bodies to understand themselves. They viewed the universe as a kind of celestial clock which chronicles man's evolution. This divination science has come to be known as astrology.

In astrology, time is not seen as linear, but cyclical. It can be measured by following the movements of the sun, moon and planets.

The moon rules our emotions, and during its 29 1/2 day journey around the earth, you experience a complete cycle within your emotional body. This cycle influences how you create in the world, and it can be broken down into eight phases, lasting roughly three and a half days each.

Here's how the moon influences your life.

New Moon

This is the beginning of the lunar cycle, and during this time we feel pulled to concentrate on a new direction, focus and theme. Pay special attention to your issues and desires at this time, for what you focus on now sets the theme for this cycle.

Crescent Moon

The moon at crescent pulls you to clarify your theme established at new moon. As you determine your next steps, you will build the necessary momentum to reach your goals. Your desires will be fueled by the will to act.

First Quarter Moon

First quarter moon urges you to act upon your new moon desires. The universe acts as well, creating circumstances in your life that help you reach your goals.

Gibbous Moon

As the moon swells to gibbous phase, you feel the pull to connect with others. This is a time to receive support for your goals, which often comes in the form of encouragement, an aid from friends and loved ones.

Take note of the people you meet at gibbous moon and the assistance they may be able to offer you.

Be open, as well, to new ideas which offer solutions to the challenges presented by your new moon theme.

Full Moon ○

    This is the time for major realizations concerning your lunar theme.
    During this phase the moon's energy is at its peak, forcing us to expand our awareness and see things more clearly.

Disseminating Moon ☾

    Now is the time to act in full awareness on your lunar theme.
    At new moon a seed is planted. At disseminating moon, it is harvested!

Last Quarter Moon

Now is the time to make a life change or changes. You've gotten a little clearer on who you are during this lunar cycle, and it's now time to release whatever appears to be holding you back from a more joyous life. It may simply be an idea or a belief that you're releasing, as you let go of all that no longer serves you.

Balsamic Moon

This is the last phase of the lunar cycle, a time for letting go of the past and looking ahead to the future. What are you thinking about these days? Interests at balsamic moon provide clues to where you're heading in the next lunar cycle and beyond. The last day of the lunar cycle, be prepared to let it all go. Tomorrow will bring a new cycle and each lunar cycle builds upon the awareness gained from the last.

New Moon Reality Creation

    The new moon phase is the prime time to check in and feel what new direction your spirit is calling you to take. Let yourself visualize what you'd like to bring into your life at this time. The inner call is to start anew... new projects, new ventures, and even a new life!

    Use this time to gain clarity on where you are going by working with the Aquarian Runes.

Reality Creation Exercise

(to be done at New Moon)

Write out what you would like to create in your life this lunar cycle.

_____
_____
_____
_____
_____
_____
_____

Now pull a rune for what you must focus on to create your desires:

notes:

Rune Lunation Layout

Draw a rune for each of the eight lunar phases to divine your next 29 1/2 day creation cycle. This layout is most powerful when done at new moon. However, you may use this layout anytime, simply find out what phase the moon is in and start your reading from there. Read counterclockwise.

notes:_____

notes:_____   New Moon   notes:_____

Crescent   Balsamic

notes:_____   notes:_____

First Qtr   Last Qtr

notes:_____   notes:_____

Gibbous   Disseminating

Full Moon

notes:_____

My Lunation Theme

My primary theme for this lunation is...

 notes:

*Note: To continue working with this system of consciously creating your reality, order a Reality Creation Workbook through Doorway Publications. The workbook includes a lunar/solar calendar and a personal journal. See the back of this book for details.

Completion

You're ready to resolve what's been holding you back. From resolution will come a new beginning. You're clearing away old beliefs and outgrown relationships, paving a way for a new life.

Going Within

    Your answers can all be found within you, and your spirit is calling you to go within to receive them.

    Spend some quiet time alone. Meditate, pray, write in a journal, or go for a walk. Do whatever it takes to calm yourself, so that you may receive guidance from the "still small voice within."

Flowing

You're flowing with the forces of divine will. You're allowing things to just happen without letting your ego get attached to a particular outcome. You're trusting that whatever is happening is always perfect, remembering that there is divine plan.

The Shadow

It's time to look at your shadow issues, (i.e., what you have been repressing). Fear, insecurity and pain are all energies that magnetize undesirable situations into your life. Look at your fears and unresolved issues, and look without selfjudgment. Just feel what you feel, and let the feelings come and go.

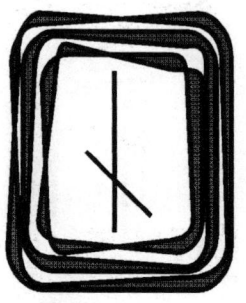

Dark Night of the Soul

A difficult passage has arisen forcing you to face your shadow issues (i.e., fears, doubts, insecurities) directly. Remembrance that you are unlimited spirit in a body is most important now. Pick another rune for guidance on how to move through this situation.

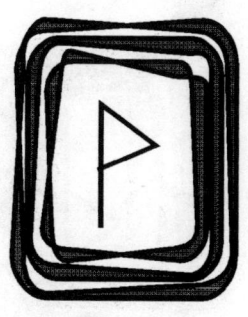

Joy

Congratulations for claiming the power you have to create the life of your choosing! This rune signifies new clarity, illumination, joy and even increased prosperity in your life. This is the reward for following your spirit without hesitation.

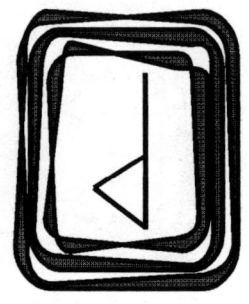

Fear

The fear that you can't have what you want surfaces, and it is time to look at this fear. Issues have arisen which are showing you what you really believe is possible, as opposed to what you want believe. Pull another rune for guidance on how you can move through your fears.

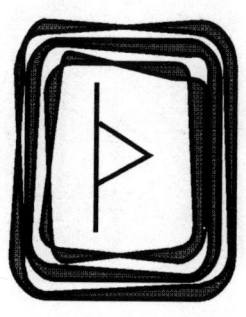

The Bridge

Walking upon your path you've now come to a bridge. Know that on the other side of this bridge is a new life, more joyous than the old. Crossing this bridge means becoming more of who you are. It means remembering you are spirit creating the life in which you live.

Contemplation

So much has happened so fast, you need time to integrate it all before making any decisions on what steps to take next.

Termination/New Beginnings

The life you've been living has outgrown its form. That form must now die to make way for a new life. It's time for changes. It's time for letting go of relationships and situations that no longer serve you.

Primary Relationship

It's time for a good hard look at your relationship with yourself, for all your other relationships are mirrors reflecting that one. Are you loving yourself enough? Are you honoring your needs? These are the questions you must ask yourself now.

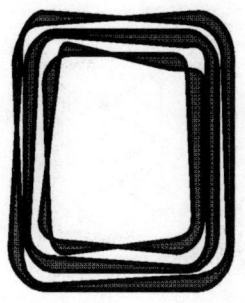

Destiny

This rune represents the unknown and the unknowable. Some things must stay hidden until the proper time so that, through your choices, you may learn the lessons you have come here to learn. However, this rune signifies the issue at hand is related to your life's destiny.

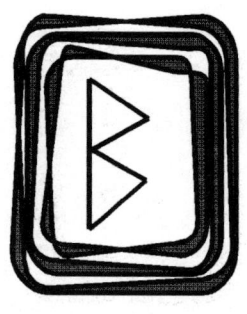

Growth

Spirit rejoices in the process of your unfoldment. As your awareness increases you may find yourself quickly outgrowing old forms, patterns and ideas that no longer serve you. Try not to be attached to anything, knowing that whatever is truly yours will always stay with you.

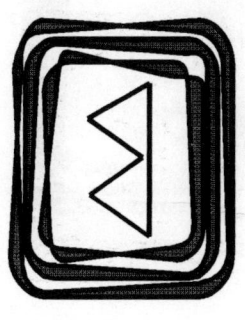

Stuck

There appears to be an obstacle to your growth. Some long held emotional or mental pattern is creating a temporary setback for you. Remember you don't need to know how to change a limiting pattern for the change to take place. Just tell the universe you are ready to change, and allow spirit to show you how.

Disconnectedness

You may be feeling disconnected to your power at this time, as a perceived limitation appears greater than your ability to overcome it. Within every problem is a gift, however a chance to transcend limitation and anchor in more of your omnipotent power. Ask the universe what you should focus on now to realign with your Self, and pull another rune for guidance.

Not Knowing

Spirit is asking you to step outside yourself for a moment into the role of an observer. Are the thoughts you are thinking coming from what you know from your own experience to be true, or are you accepting at face value what others have told you? Claim your power by allowing yourself to be empty and not know. Through that void your spirit's wisdom can guide you into divine right action.

Inner Communication

This rune signifies the need to open up the channel of communication between your ego and your spirit. You can tell when this channel is open because you don't second-guess your actions. When you do what feels right in the moment you allow your spirit to be the guiding force in your life. Each action you do then is perfect for the moment, creating only divine outcomes.

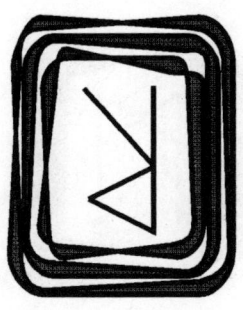

Outer Communication

You may find it difficult communicating with certain people at this time as you move more into your true self. Conflicts may arise with those who are holding onto an old, outgrown image of you. Let others be where they need to be, but stand firm in your own self-perception. As you accept the new you, others will also.

Self-nurturance

This is a time of major growth and change, and it is important now to take time out to nurture your inner child. The child within you may be feeling insecure with all the changes your adult self is making. Give yourself a rest. Treat yourself. Relax and be playful. If fears arise, acknowledge them, and ask your spirit to help you release them in a loving way.

Old Habits

Past habits are sometimes difficult to break. The counsel here is "don't rush your own process." Be your own best friend and allow yourself to be slow in resolving the issues that take more time to resolve than you'd like. Remember all things happen in divine time. Let it be OK not to know, and wait for guidance from spirit.

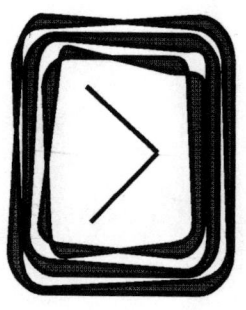

Death

You're experiencing a death of a way of life invalidated by your growth. A relationship may be dying or some aspect of yourself that is no longer appropriate to the you, you are becoming. This time calls for gladly giving up the old.

Opening

    You are opening to new ideas, new people and new clarity. Now is a time of opportunity as your energy is indicating to spirit that you're ready to receive divine direction to embark on a new path. Now is the time to claim the ability you have to become a -knower-, one who knows his or her destiny and acts accordingly.

Movement

Now is the time to act, and you know what to do. Your spirit is pulling you in a particular direction. Follow your bliss.

Hold Off

The rune's counsel is to hold off on action, at least temporarily. The right door has not yet opened and all the facts aren't in. Be patient and wait on spirit's will. What's yours will come to you.

Messages

The universe is speaking to you through signs and signals, indicating which way you should go. You have seen or are seeing the signs, and you need now to acknowledge them.

Subconscious

What is unknown or hidden, within your subconscious desires, now to become known. It's time for you to acknowledge some part of yourself you have not wanted to see before. Acknowledge it, feel it and love it.

Wholeness

    This is the path to wholeness. This is the path to light. This is the path to who you are. This is the pathway home.

    Whatever the question is, this rune indicates the answer is "yes." The green light is on, and the call is to "go for it!"

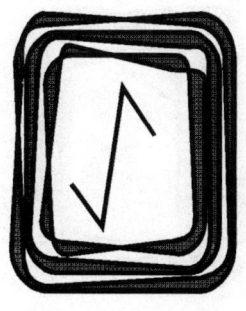

Limitation

There appears to be an obstacle in your way, but it is only an illusion. As long as you perceive it, you will grow from it so that you become stronger. When you have no more need of this obstacle, it will disappear.

Fulfillment

You feel the joy of receiving and having. You're letting yourself receive without blocking the flow.

Remember the secret to staying in this joyous space of receptivity is gratitude. Gratitude is an energy which opens the heart, and an open heart is a receptive one.

Deserving

It's becoming clear to you now that what you have is in accordance with what you believe you deserve. To have more you must now look at your beliefs about money, possessions, relationships and happiness.

(note: The Aquarian Runes can help you change limiting beliefs. Refer to the Guided Questions section of this book, under Changing Limiting Beliefs - P. 28)

Breakthrough

After feeling stuck in self doubt or fear you've made a significant breakthrough. You can now move more easily in the direction of your desires.

Radical Discontinuity

Spirit says "absolutely no more" to the old way. A situation that needs changing is now being forced upon you. The traditional term for this rune is hail, and often the energy associated with it feels quite stormy. However, it forces changes which must occur. Expect abrupt endings, important disassociations and so forth.

Right Direction

This is it, the right path for you! You know this is the right path because it feels right. Your ego's in check and your spirit is in the driver's seat. It feels joyous following your divine path. Keep doing what you love, and the blessings will follow.

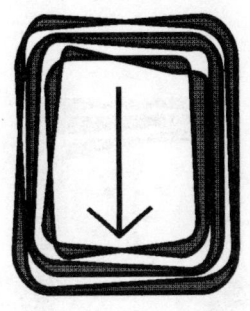

Ego Conflicts

It's time for a good hard look at your motives here. Are you getting attached to a particular outcome? Is your spirit asking you to shift directions and you're resisting? Remember not to judge yourself at this time for anything you're feeling. This rune suggests that what your ego would like to do may not be your highest path. It's time to realign with your spirit. Pull another rune for guidance on how to do this.

Partnership

The energy of connectedness surrounds you. You're joining with others with an open heart, realizing that love is always the answer to any problem. The counsel is to keep working on unconditionally loving yourself, for the more you love and accept yourself the more you can do so with others.

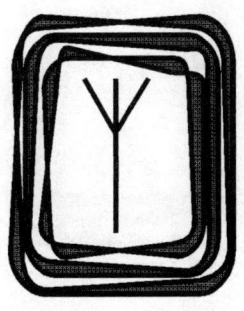

Eyes Open

Spirit is asking you to look at your life with open eyes, and not be afraid to acknowledge what you see. Your perceptions don't have to be "right" to anyone else. They are valid for you and you must acknowledge them, even if what you see is different as supposed to how others see things.

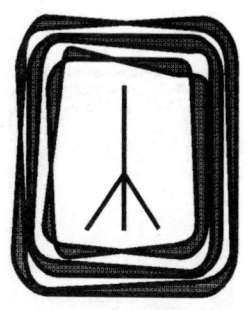

Mirrors

Look carefully at the associations you're making at this time. Like energies attract, and nothing happens to you except in accord with your own state of consciousness. Those around you have been drawn to you through the law of resonance. If someone is doing or saying something to you that you don't like, ask yourself honestly, "What is this reflecting within me?"

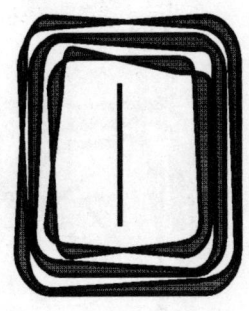

Stand Still

It's time to realize the value of action which is actionless. It's time to receive the clarity that comes from standing still and listening to the voice within.

Harvest

When you're doing what you love, you can only prosper. This rune signifies beneficial outcomes. The counsel is to hold fast to your vision of what you'd like to achieve, and go for it! Your spirit is behind you on this one.

Let Go

Your spirit has said "enough," and will no longer let you walk a path that is not your own. Often an allegiance to an ideal, belief or relationship is the hardest thing to release. However, you must release something now.

The Cocoon

You're like a caterpillar transforming into a butterfly. Deep changes are taking place within you now, and it's hard at this time to put your feelings into words. Flow with the process.

Tools for a New World...

Create Heaven on Earth
with the vision of
The 11:11 Alignment Cards

Unveil the vastness of your true Self.

This divination tool is uplifting and inspiring, reminding us of our angelic and starry heritage.

Set includes 73 glossy, white cards, printed in gold and blue. Affirmations on back of each card, plus instruction booklet.

$ 15

Tools for a New World . . .

Crystal Rune Set

Enhance your rune readings
with the power of

Genuine Quartz Crystals

This handpainted rune set comes in your choice of:

❈ *Adventurine Quartz Crystal,
   for promoting inner peace and
   a positive outlook on life*

   ❈ *Rose Quartz Crystal,
      for opening your heart
      to greater self-love
      and self-fullfillment*

Includes Velvet Pouch $ 35

Tools for a new world . . .

Personal Astrology Report
Receive Guidance From the Stars

"The Sky within" is a computerized 15-20 page reading of your life.

Written by well-known astrologer Steven Forrest.

✹ Perfect for newcomers to Astrology

✹ A great tool for self-exploration

$ 25

Reality Creation Workbook
Create the Life of Your Dreams

This workbook is based on the reality creation system in the Aquarian Runes.

Includes calendar with exact lunar phase dates, divination layouts and personal journal.

$ 12

Order Form

ORDERED BY:
Your Name: _____
Street Address: _____
City: _____ State: _____ Zip: _____
Phone: _____

Ship to: If different from ordered by
Name: _____
Street Address: _____
City: _____ State: _____
Zip: _____

Send this form to:
Doorway Publications
16428 Tee Place
Weed, CA 96094
or call toll free
1-800-765-9823

Payment:
Check ☐ C.O.D ☐ Moneyorder ☐
Visa ☐ Mastercard ☐
Card # _____ Exp.Date: _____
Cardholder's Signature:
_____

VISA

Quantity	Item	Price	Total Price
	11:11 Alignment Cards	$ 15	
	Adventurine Rune Set	$ 35	
	Rose Quartz Rune Set	$ 35	
	Personal Astrology Report	$ 25	
	Reality Creation Workbook	$ 12	
Shipping & Handling $ 2.90 for first item + $ .50 for each addl. item		Total Amount of order	
		Shipping & Handling	
		In CA add 7.25 % Tax	
		Total Amount	

If ordering an astrology report, please include your name along with date, place and time of birth.